THE RELIGIOUS LIFE TODAY

Also by Karl Rahner
and published by Burns & Oates

SACRAMENTUM MUNDI (Editor)
ENCYCLOPEDIA OF THEOLOGY: A CONCISE SACRAMENTUM
MUNDI (Editor)
A CONCISE THEOLOGICAL DICTIONARY (with Vorgrimler)
WATCH AND PRAY WITH ME
THE CHURCH AND THE SACRAMENTS
ENCOUNTERS WITH SILENCE
CHRISTIAN AT THE CROSSROADS
BIBLICAL HOMILIES
EVERYDAY FAITH
GRACE IN FREEDOM
SERVANTS OF THE LORD
THE TRINITY
THE ETERNAL YEAR
CELEBRATION OF THE EUCHARIST (with Häussling)
THE CHRISTIAN OF THE FUTURE
VISIONS AND PROPHECIES
HOMINISATION
ON THE THEOLOGY OF DEATH
REVELATION AND TRADITION (with Ratzinger)
THE DYNAMIC ELEMENT IN THE CHURCH
ON HERESY
INSPIRATION AND THE BIBLE
THE EPISCOPATE AND THE PRIMACY (with Ratzinger)
CHURCH IN TRANSITION
MEDITATIONS ON HOPE AND LOVE

The Religious Life Today

Karl Rahner

BURNS &OATES LONDON

First published in Great Britain in 1976 by
Burns & Oates Ltd
2-10 Jerdan Place London SW6 5PT

This translation was made by V. Green

Printed and bound in Great Britain by
Billing & Sons Limited, Guildford,
London and Worcester

ISBN 0 86012 028 7

Contents

1 The setting of the religious life: The Christian message now

The Christian message has to be discussed again. That is not so strange as it seems. After all, even those who think of themselves as Christians and have institutional ties with a Christian Church can't agree about its basic content. But then we have to try to explain the discrepancy between the desire to be a Christian and a member of a Christian Church and what seems to be an almost total difference among Christians in interpreting their Christianity. Is that common desire to belong to Christianity and a Church simply a matter of the traditions and other attractions of social institutions with a long and rich past? Or does it reflect a shared conviction beneath diverse interpretations?

A single understanding of the Christian message is something we feel we have to try to reach. But perhaps the reason for our striving isn't its non-existence. Perhaps we have to reach that unity of understanding because it does exist, though possibly below the surface.

Somehow, somewhere, a statement of the Christian message has to be made. It must express the fundamental Christian beliefs which we hope unite us now, despite all denominational disputes. That can't be done by leaving out or glossing over controversial theological views.

What is required is an attempt to restate the basic religious conviction below the level of theological dispute, which gives ground for hope that agreement will be possible even on matters of contention, once we have rediscovered together the very basis of the Christian message.

That is all the more urgent because today doctrinal differences exist not only between individual Churches, each with its own totally homogeneous and unanimously accepted interpretation of the content of the Christian message, but are fully developed within each Church.

The need for a statement

A statement of the content of the Christian message is necessary. It is necessary because what makes the unity of a Church is not a technical organization for the satisfaction of religious needs, but a common creed. A Church can only be a missionary Church when it can say what unites and moves it. The Churches can only carry out their ministry to the world together when they can show the world that they pursue their mission as a result of a shared religious conviction: a conviction by which the world can assess the common activity of the Churches.

On the other hand, while searching for this one fundamental confession of faith we must realize that such a creed can be based on a very wide range of starting-points and display very different features. That follows from the complexity of Christian history, with its multiplicity of traditions; from the wide range of

Christian theologies; and from the highly-nuanced intellectual situation in which a Christian creed has to be formulated and received. There may even be more than one basic formulation of the Christian faith. Different formulations need not be so divergent as to split the Church, nor must they necessarily be transcended in a single form of words, provided that two criteria are observed. Firstly, there must be no weakening of the insistence that human beings are totally dependent on Jesus for an historical assurance of their 'salvation' (however we are to understand that word). Secondly (for there is no other way in which dependence on Jesus is possible), the historical transmission of our dependence on Jesus must be recognized as fundamental and essential.

A statement in history

When making our basic statement about the Christian message, we must remember that it has to speak to the real situation of those to whom it is addressed, and that this situation, individual and collective, is part of history and therefore constantly changing.

Of course the belief that the Christian message will always find hearers (subject to the messenger's fidelity and the incalculable arrangements of the Lord of history) is a fundamental part of the message. On the other hand, that implies that the Christian message must take more than superficial account of the actual situation of its hearers, and that it can do so without endangering its essential meaning.

An important criterion of a true and life-giving orthodoxy of the Christian message is its ability to do more than monotonously repeat old formulas. Monotony

3

would show that it took no account of the historical transformation of its hearers' situation. Much that is officially regarded in the Church as suitable for the proclamation of the Christian message today doesn't satisfy that criterion.

The content of the message

The message must say something about God. If it doesn't, it isn't a Christian message. Nor would it be a message for us now if it started (as it has on the whole until now) from Thomas Aquinas's belief that everyone knows what 'God' means, and that the most that has to be done is to demonstrate his existence and the nature of his relation to the world. What 'God' means is deeply obscure, and many of the ideas the word conjures up are wrong and a constant cause of atheism. Much more thought than in the past must be given to ways in which we can talk intelligibly about God so as to make our message credible. The main object of this rethinking must be straight-forward preaching.

Even relatively short statements about the Christian message probably ought to make explicit reference to the basis of our knowledge of God.

Its nature enables and its contemporary situation obliges the Christian message to make its statement of God's saving involvement with the world and history (which culminates in Jesus) within the framework of a universal history of salvation and revelation. That framework is not an addition to, but an integral part of the statement. The eschatological event of Jesus Christ must be seen within this history and as its highest point. Only hindsight enables us to see Old Testament history

4

as the direct prehistory and immediate setting of the Christ-event. (In this respect even the approach of Vatican II's *Verbum Dei* is, from a kerygmatic — or 'preaching' — viewpoint, outdated.)

A Christian message can't see Jesus just as the *bearer of a message*. It has to proclaim him as the *content of the message*. To that extent the content of the traditional Chalcedonian Christology of the incarnate Word — the Logos — may remain true and binding. But that doesn't mean that simply repeating it as the whole content or the beginning of a contemporary confession of faith in Jesus Christ will satisfy the requirement of historical adequacy.

Let me put it another way. We may say that in Jesus Christ total acceptance of God's giving of himself to the world, understood as our hope and absolute future, the absolute depth and responsibility of our love for each other, and so on, attained its irrevocable finality. We have now, in another form, and one which is perhaps more accessible to us today, expressed what traditional Christology teaches as dogma, provided that these statements are understood with the full weight of all their implications and are not taken as mythology in the bad sense.

In expressing the importance of Jesus for our salvation we must aim at the greatest possible unity of Christological and soteriological — or salvific — statements. The causal relation of Jesus's suffering and death to our salvation can be understood by analogy with the causality of sacramental signs. Jesus's fate proclaims and prefigures our salvation by making the saving will of God present in history with eschatological irrevocabil-

5

ity. In that sense, it does what it signifies, and at the same time gets its effect from what it signifies. If these statements are acceptable, we can make the meaning of Jesus's death intelligible for ourselves today without detracting from the dogmas, and without having to turn to conceptual models which people nowadays would find mythological and excessively anthropomorphic.

Starting from there, our message would have to go on to say something about *the Church* as the *community of those who believe the message of Jesus*. We would have to make clear that such a community must have an institutional life in society in order to do justice to human nature and to the reality which it is the community's purpose to proclaim. We would have to make clear that such an institution has to be accepted as historically contingent in many of its features and yet as above history; we would have to show that the greatest possible clarity about the continuity of the history of this institution guarantees its origin in Jesus, provided that the truth of the past is confirmed by the courage to face a new future.

2 The religious life today and tomorrow

If we members of religious orders are convinced of the value of our life as Christians, and if we have the courage to acknowledge the life we undertook when we made our vows in the Church to Jesus, we are making the best possible provision for the future. How many will come after us we do not know. The future existence of religious orders depends ultimately on our being today the people we should be. We have given much thought to the essence of religious life in meditation, reflexion and lectures. We have prayed about it. We have constantly told God that we wish to be, and to be more proficiently, what we are.

But we need to think about our vocation again and again. As long as the quiet confidence of being what we are grows in some hearts, it is enough. A seed is sown for the future. The more we are who we want and ought to be, the more chance, prospect and hope we have that our religious life in the Church will not merely hold its ground or survive, but will serve God, men and therefore the Church.

1 Essential Christianity
In the formal decree on the Church and in the apostolic

constitution *Lumen Gentium*, Vatican II expressly states that the religious life is characteristic of the Church: not in the same way as office — the ministry — but in another equally decisive way. The religious life does not belong to the Church in the sense that we claim to be better or 'real' Christians. Those who love the most vividly, believe the most loyally and hope the most strongly are the best Christians — the decisive ones. God knows in the distribution of his grace where that sort of Christianity is at work; it is found at all levels of Christianity and in all Christian vocations.

According to the demands of Vatican II, what Christianity ought to be should be alive and evident in the religious life: ultimate faith, hope and love; faith in eternal life, hope in the absolute future, which is God, and a love which is the love of God and one's neighbour in absolute unity.

What is 'essential Christianity'? We could say simply: hope. Hope that this frightful, sombre, apparently hopeless event called life will have a happy issue. Christianity is hope. Christianity is love of one's neighbour, and a love of one's neighbour which draws its ultimate strength from liberating contemplation of the crucified and risen Jesus. Through all these experiences we come to know what is meant when we say 'God'. Only if, in all the gloominess of life, we hope in an ultimate, beatific meaning and end to life; only if we try to love our neighbour selflessly; only if we meet the crucified and risen Jesus; only then do we ultimately know who is meant by this word 'God'. Otherwise we must imagine that the word refers to some strange being or an empty camouflage which we use without knowing its purpose.

This essential Christianity can't stay at the level of theory in people's heads or of Sunday sermons, but has to become life — immediate, realistic and habitual — at the heart of the 'secular' daily round. It is there that hope, faith, love and loyalty to one's neighbour must be loved.

Other people fulfil these demands as much as we do, perhaps even exemplarily. None of these things is a privilege we can arrogate to ourselves alone. We have, however, professed this ultimate meaning of life. Precisely because these supreme ideals must become tangible in our lives, we wish to some extent to organize and institutionalize them in the everyday way we live. We want them to become practice in a Church in which there are people who testify that they hope, that they live the life of a love which stands fast without despairing even when life is drawn into the incomprehensibility of the fate of the crucified Jesus.

Those people shape the Church and cause the Church to become a sign of hope, a symbol of love, and a call to responsibility for one's neighbour. Religious should be numbered among those people who wish to give their testimony in the Church in this way: simply and practically, without empty words, in the activity of life. As Vatican II says, they should be a sign of what the Church should be for the world: a proclamation, a constant confirmation and attestation of the fact that in the final analysis the world is saved in God's power, in God's love, in God's faithfulness, in God's mercy, in God's paradisal future.

It goes without saying that we do not ascribe to ourselves the privilege of being the only people who are signs of the Church. Anyone who faithfully and self-lessly does his duty in life: a mother who makes sacrifices for her children, an invalid whom death stares hopelessly in the face and who yet takes shelter, in confident surrender, in the hands of the incomprehensible God; all these are as it were members of the Church confessing Jesus Christ, witnesses of what the Church should be, bearers of the Church's rôle, a signal of hope for the salvation of the world in a world which, despite all the great achievements of which it can boast today, keeps its sombre aspect. We claim no exclusive privilege. We have no exclusive vocation.

Why, however, should we religious not say: We want to serve our neighbour in word, deed, love, loyalty, care, selflessness and prayer, in our own way as God has granted it to us, and in so far as it is necessary, beneficial and useful to the world, whether we are alone in this or not? If others do it differently — well, God lavishes his grace, his gifts, as he will; they will be blessed. But we claim the right to do it in our own way. It is not true that the world could do without this activity, this witness, at the very least not of those who serve the sick and dying, the poor and the orphan. The world will be the sooner convinced that there is something apart from secret egotism and war on existence, that there are and can be such things as love, faith, and hope in eternal life.

2 Religious life and change

It is a truism that religious life is changing. All religious notice it: their numbers are falling, their work load is increasing. They find themselves asking what works they must abandon as their various activities are reorganized to accommodate reduced manpower. This change, which all orders are experiencing more or less harshly as a crisis or even as a threat to their own self-consciousness as religious Christians, has to be integrated into the general change taking place in the Church as a whole and often in forms which we find less than gratifying, or which horrify us, or which are uncomfortable for us, or which force us into unaccustomed paths.

The changes in religious life are only a part of the change in the Church which, viewed as a whole, is necessary. Because the world changes, the Church must change with it if it is to remain itself, if, that is, it is to remain the ambassador of the living God, of his gifts and his grace, because otherwise it could no longer be heard and understood. If we really belong to the Church and have to share its mission and mandate, it is self-evident that in a world of rapid change, and therefore in a necessarily changing Church, things cannot stay the same in religious life. Other and new forms of religious life will perhaps emerge. Orders will have to evolve a new life-style, perhaps more 'individualistic' and 'anti-authoritarian' and in some sense, seen from without, more secular, more consistent with the life-style of modern man, who has 'come of age'.

The fact remains that there will always be people in the Church who come together, renouncing marriage, for a common work in the service of their neighbour, out of love for the crucified Jesus and in the hope of eternal life. There will always be people (because there is no other way of doing things) who organize, institutionalize, plan, put into action such a common service, in distributing the various tasks that satisfy a common aim. In other words, as long as there are Christians, there will be religious, even in a changed world, even with a changed style of religious life.

That doesn't mean that we have to dismantle the old orders. It has always been shown in the history of the Church that the old orders can take on a new lease of life, even though perhaps in a changed form, side by side with recently founded orders. For example, the French Benedictines of the seventeenth and eighteenth centuries were splendid, flourishing, vital, although it could have been said that the characteristic order of that period was the Society of Jesus. The seventeenth- and eighteenth-century Dominicans enjoyed a splendid new vitality, although they were already a very old order by then.

The idea, then, that new times need new orders does not at all mean that the old orders must necessarily be so rheumatic and unadaptable that they cannot hope to keep up with the times. There must evidently be in these old orders a certain reappraisal in the light of the new requirements and the old tradition, but there is no *a priori* reason why such a tension should not be worked out fruitfully and successfully. The person who denies a past is not the person most suitable for a future; on the contrary, the person who tries to master the future's new challenge with an undimmed insight into his past will win the greater future.

Religious life will change, even in the 'old' orders. That doesn't mean, as far as the individual is concerned, that he must be despondent when he has the impression that his own order is responding to the force of circumstances more slowly than according to his ideas it should. In any community there are bound to be those who step on the gas and those who apply the brake, and they must all possess that love for each other and for their common service in which such tensions between 'traditionalists' and 'progressivists' are sustained. It is also part of a rational, selfless person's maturity to adapt himself, serve, love and be faithful wherever he finds himself in a situation which he does not always find to his liking, or which he would not have thought up in his own ideas and plans for the future. The same is surely true of family life: there are older and younger people, and different tendencies. If a family is healthy and vital, it can cope with such tensions. If the younger members of a religious institution are intent only on raising the dust and the older members only on lamenting the good old days, both sides show merely that they do not have the proper spirit appropriate to an order: the spirit of selfless love.

That spirit demands that we understand, accept and tolerate the gifts and particular abilities of others, even though we might not appreciate them at first. When Paul, in 1 Corinthians (chapter 12) and other letters, expressly instructs Christians that there is one Spirit in the Church and yet many gifts and functions and members in that one Church, it goes without saying that the diversity of gifts necessarily brings with it difficulties in mutual understanding. If I absolutely understood the other person in his own particular personality, I should have his gifts. In reality, however, I do not possess them, or at least not in the same way, and I must learn to co-exist with him, to share with him the loving unity of the

13

one community. Such behaviour is not, of course, exclusive to the Christian: every rational, selfless, well-intentioned person needs it. If religious can't manage this love-inspired toleration in the tensions and changes of today within a religious community, it's high time to make themselves scarce in the Church and in the world.

These new times, with their inevitable change even in religious life, give ample opportunity for mutual responsibility, mutual love, and in my opinion also for what we call, in somewhat emotive religious language, sharing Christ's cross. As Christians we have confessed this cross; daily we celebrate the Lord's death in the Eucharist. Now there are certainly situations in human life in which we directly feel man's relationship to the mystery of Christ's cross. We should, however, soberly and objectively discover and accept Christ's cross in our everyday lives: where we bear with each other; where we must and should persevere without exactly knowing the outcome; where we make a stand and, as Paul says, 'hope against hope'; where our fellows perhaps smile at us as old-fashioned and yet cheerfully accept our service. This cross of Christ extends very 'anonymously', very unexplicitly, very unemotively, in a very everyday fashion, over our lives. If we can find it there, we shall also manage to endure with resignation and even cheerful hope, the change, the insecurity, the aggression suffered by a religious community today.

3   The life-style of a nursing nun

There are people today, both modern pagans and not a few Christians, who think that the real essence of Christianity, once we've discarded the obsolete padding,

14

is a realistic, profane, secular love of one's neighbour and obligation to other men. The life of a nursing nun can demonstrate in its own way that there is a love of God and Jesus which precisely frees and qualifies man for love of his neighbour, on occasions, in work and in menial daily services in which no one now doubts that one can do it joyfully and make sense of it only if something mysteriously nameless, which is precisely what we call love of God and Jesus, lives in this person.

This remarkable war between attention to one's neighbour and a genuine relationship to God which is smouldering or even openly raging in the theology and practice of the Church today is in the last analysis meaningless, because the two things belong indissolubly to each other from the first. Only the person who knows what is meant by God really loves his neighbour, and the ultimate meaning, the ultimate strength of this love for one's neighbour emerges only from this love for the mysteriously incomprehensible God.

By her life, and not by pious or abstract theory, a nursing nun can demonstrate that God and the neighbour belong together in a way which we in Christianity are slowly and rightly learning for the first time, although it was already more than clear in Jesus and in John's teaching (1 John 3: 18-24; 4: 7-15). What we must learn is not an either/or between a relationship to the one we call God and a relationship to man, but a unity of heart, of activity, of love, of service, a unity in which both God and the neighbour are given together and grow together and are intelligible only together in the most mysterious way.

If the life of a nursing sister realizes this unity with

the help of God's grace over a lifetime, without anxious inquiry into the chances of success, her life contains something which today belongs to the things which are absolutely necessary to the Church. Everywhere in the Church there are people anxiously asking: What must we as Christians do? What do we have to do to live a Christianity which is really worthy of the name, which really has to do with Jesus and not only with erudite, abstract theology? When these people say: What is wanted is service, responsibility, faithfulness to one's neighbour, taking one's neighbour seriously, getting out of oneself so that in the end one is really with the other, not again egotistically with oneself, it needs to be pointed out by some authentic, genuine, vital Christian that love of God and love of neighbour are really one commandment on which Christianity is centred. That way is not the only style, the only method of such a life. In the life of a nursing nun, however, one can, by allowing one's neighbour access in one's own life, truly live out what Christianity and human life are actually about. And they are about loving people and so coming to know that one has in this way, in some mysterious fashion, already bestowed one's heart on that ineffable mystery who embraces us, who wants to take us and our lives and our infinite future to himself in love.

The person who loves his neighbour knows who God is; otherwise not; otherwise he has perhaps erudite words and ideas about God, but not God himself. The life of a nursing nun can really be the wonderful experience, the improbable adventure of a person who says: I will lavish my heart on others, not in feelings and talk but 'as something real and active' (1 John 3.18), in the sober bitterness of life, I will see for once whether in this way I shall find and grasp what God is. Nursing nuns have begun just such a wonderful adventure in all the soberness of daily life. Why should they not continue? The road leads straight on. The future is perhaps not very far distant: the future, that is, in which for once we really succeed in losing our hearts to our neighbour and so to God. If we examine our hearts from this point of view and do not deceive ourselves, it so often seems as though they are wandering by endless paths on which a great deal happens only to end up despairingly where they started: at our own egotism. It is a difficult adventure to try really to love one's neighbour so that one does not return to oneself but finds one's neighbour, God, and so, for the first time, oneself too.

Something else belongs to the 'mystery' of a nursing nun's life. She deals with the human mystery of sickness and death. Naturally, in the daily routine it is necessarily sprinkled with the dust of habit. It becomes something which one cannot allow to approach too closely if one's heart is not to be too rapidly and falsely crushed by the frightfulness of everyday life. Nursing nuns, however, still have to deal with sickness and death in their lives. Even in today's world that is an ineffable mystery.

Nursing nuns have to deal with this mystery. They must be intimate with it. Not only in the daily routine, however. They must be and increasingly become people who despite all the habit of it really manage not to run away, to stay with it. By their calling they stand close to the mystery of sickness and death. One can become hard in a false way in an effort to bear the incomprehensible pain. May God give all nursing nuns the grace to be so loving and sympathetic that they can stand at a sick-bed or a death-bed not only bodily and not only with the techniques of modern medicine, but as persons who suffer the unspeakable mystery of sickness and death with other people and who accompany these people in a real, human way to the extent that, because another person stands at their bedside with an open, human heart, the sick retain the hope (even though they perhaps cannot reflect on it) that this dark abyss threatening to swallow them up is the abyss of the mystery of God, the abyss of grace, the abyss of eternal life. They must be the people to accompany the sick and the dying as far as possible along that road with loving care and fidelity.

Isn't that a vocation that will still be necessary tomorrow? I don't say that it can be fulfilled only by religious Christians. I do say, however, that it *can* be fulfilled by them. And that is still a sacred calling which one can accept from God day by day in love and faithfulness. It makes excessive demands on one's heart, which seems not to find in its emptiness and narrowness and poverty and need for love the strength to be able to give others in the darkness of their illness and death something other than the ministrations of mere medicine with all its technique and heartless learning. It will always make excessive demands. But the fact that, by God's grace, a little love, a little help, a little responsibility wells up — we ourselves do not know how or whence — from the pit, as it were, of our empty hearts, can and should be the business and responsibility of the life which the nursing nuns lead. Furthermore, the nuns should, by God's grace, live and experience it as a gift from God in which one almost ashamedly avows: I cannot by my own strength, but I can — incomprehensibly — in the strength of someone else. It is then called grace. Loving the other, not only theoretically on Sundays but in the reality of life, where, for example, one takes food or makes a bed, gives a smile to one person and a cheery word to another, is what constitutes service of one's suffering neighbour. The sick then feel safe somewhere, even in their loneliness and isolation. They feel a security which is not ultimately that given by the nurse, but the security which the one we call God gives through her because the love of the eternal God goes out to the other in her so-called love of her neighbour, so that they can lay hold of it even in the darkness and tiredness and emptiness and exhaustion of illness and death.

Because the religious life is a holy mission and a grace for us in our faith, hope and love, it has a significance even for 'tomorrow'. As Paul says (Gal. 6.14), the only thing we can boast about is the cross of our Lord Jesus Christ. We boast about the grace which God has lavished on us. We are humbled in this boasting of God's grace given to us, because we never live up to it. We have the right, however, indeed we have the sacred duty, the holy possibility, of boasting of God's grace and saying: we are and wish to be those who love, who serve, who are selfless and so experience God himself in his own beatitude.

So our religious life, which we confess as our 'today', becomes the proclamation of the hope and the belief

19

that God will still grant that life to people in the Church, if there is still a Church, that is, a confession of Jesus Christ crucified and risen, in the future. We need no sociological predictions as to how many will be religious. If there is Christianity now and also in the future, because this light shed by the confession of the crucified and risen Jesus has not gone out in this world, there will also be people who organize this one love for God and men (in belief in the crucified and risen Jesus and in the hope of eternal life) into a somehow practicable, tangible form. And that means there will be some kind of religious life.

4 The modernity of daily life

To be modern or not to be modern is a very problematical question. Perhaps the person who is not modern today is the person who is modern for tomorrow. What we often pursue in the Church as highly modern is the discarded clothing of someone from yesterday which we don and in which we feel particularly modern.

Modern or not, Jesus and his life which ended in death, the bitterness of existence which no technology can overcome, these are ever-present realities. They are therefore, alas or thanks be to God, always modern. And nursing nuns face up to, do not hide from, go out to meet, wish to face squarely in the strength of Christ's cross, in the strength of the sacred hope of eternal life, in the grace of God's Spirit, this reality of life: one's neighbour in his need, responsibility for one's neighbour, the mystery of death and sickness in us and our neighbour, this reality which is always modern because it is daily and will still be daily tomorrow.

This life is good, is holy, is — rightly understood — modern; it serves our neighbour. Why should we not continue, in a way appropriate for today, evidently, not as people did hundreds of years ago? Why should we not persevere, even in 'hope against hope'? We must surrender to God and his providence the future we cannot manipulate or calculate. He will call to such a life those whom he has chosen in the future too. And that is enough for them, for the world in time to come and for us.

I maintain that we can be religious and remain religious with the confidence of the level-headed man who knows the world and yet confesses Christ crucified and risen. Nursing nuns have every reason in God's grace to be and remain nursing nuns, because they have a wonderful chance of serving their neighbour and so of finding God. And what more will a person achieve in life if he has no foolish illusions about life? If nursing nuns manage that in their lives, they have done, suffered and experienced the only thing that lasts, for they will have practised the love which 'does not come to an end' (1 Cor. 13.8).

3 Calling and vocation

In order to talk about 'calling', 'vocation' and especially vocation to the religious life (understood as a divine call) in a relatively short space, a great deal must be presumed from other sources. I suppose, for example, that man has received a divine call which is a gratuitous gift from God and a mission for man, which summons him in Jesus to his salvation and enables him to achieve it, so that all important moments of a person's life, and above all of a Christian's, in which he receives and works out his salvation, are included in that one call of election. I therefore presume that every 'calling' (in the usual sense) is included in that one call and consequently can and must be understood as a divine vocation, provided only that such a calling is explicitly or inclusively chosen as one such moment in a divine vocation to salvation in Jesus Christ.

I also suppose that such a divine vocation to a particular calling in which one follows God's call comprises several factors: pre-given inclinations, an actual life-situation with its necessities and pressures, and free choice which selects to the best of its ability from a perhaps narrow range of possibilities offered in such a way that one's own possibilities in life are developed as

23

fully as they can be and one's own salvation is therefore achieved as certainly and fully as possible.

I also assume that a vocation to the religious life, even though not exclusively, but in a special way, arises from a divine call to salvation. It does so in a special way because its content and special characteristics, in themselves and without reference to a particular person, are, as faith testifies, a genuine aspect of the one common call of man from God and to God, and because they cannot meaningfully be chosen without an explicit reference to that one common divine call of man to his salvation.

Yet for most people in their choice of calling, that reference is either not explicit at all or takes effect only at the very margin of their decisions; or else the distinction between several possible callings of a worldly nature can have so minimal a reference to the will to respect a divine call in general, or to a particular individual, that from the point of view of a 'Christian' choice of calling the distinction may be neglected.

Presuming all this, I may now attempt to say something about the call to a religious vocation and about that vocation itself, something about which there is often not sufficient clarity in the minds of religious, something perhaps too on which theologians are not fully agreed. It is usually said that a vocation to the religious life, the calling of a person to the religious life by God's gracious will, is present when: the person in question is suitable for an order, given that order's particular ministry and the obligations it imposes on its members; that order is chosen for genuinely good, 'supernatural' motives and not for worldly and egotistical reasons; and that decision to join an order is accepted by the competent authorities of the religious community.

As a general rule, it is enough if these three conditions of a genuine religious vocation are satisfied, even though in some cases it is not easy to establish whether each of the conditions (particularly the first and second) is fulfilled and even though it can subsequently transpire that it was not in fact fulfilled when the solemn vows were made. But we may still hold that over and above these three criteria of genuineness for a religious vocation, something like a real 'attraction' to a religious vocation through God's grace is necessary and desirable, even though a 'call' in this sense must not be throught of in too 'mystic' a way or as a miraculous illumination and inspiration, like the call of a prophet.

Man's freedom is not unlimited, but only a moment in the course and shape of life determined by many other aspects which elude his free control. That does not mean that someone who has chosen his religious vocation and made 'eternal vows' in the abovementioned conditions knows for certain that, provided that he does not later take culpable steps against his vocation, he can and must remain for ever in his vocation by God's will and therefore because of God's call.

Even when the conditions for a genuine vocation to enter an order are fulfilled, it can later become apparent that the preconditions of a vocation are no longer present, and the person leaves his order at peace with it and the Church. It can be the case that from the point of view of God and the conduct of one's life (which one can never completely foresee), the religious vocation was only 'for a time', although that was not the

25

intention at the beginning and the vows made were 'eternal'. The official dispensation from the obligations of the order is then no more than the ecclesial confirmation that in this particular case the genuine call from God through a religious order now leads back to another way of life. (Naturally this does not exclude the fact that official dispensation can be culpably extorted or obtained by deception. How matters then stand with the dispensation in God's eyes is a question into which I cannot go here.)

The meaning of a religious life vocation 'for life' and of 'eternal' vows can therefore consist only in the obligation of religious to shape and conduct their lives to the best of their ability in such a way that, in so far as it depends on their own freedom, they verify the three conditions, and the will to continue in the order remains conscious and firm, that is, a daily undertaking. Everything else can be left to God and his providence, which we can never definitely precalculate. Religious life is also a history which, like the life-history and vocation-history of other people, is never totally under our control.

We religious must and may (it is still a grace, of course) do all that is possible for genuine and meaningful freedom to ensure that our lives retain and keep intact for a lifetime the once-chosen shape and the internal and external constancy of a human and above all a religious life. We must never forget that when renunciation, self-denial, disappointments – in short the 'cross' – come on us unexpectedly in religious life, they are not yet signs that we have taken a false road, but, at least until proof of the contrary, are to be taken as perfectly normal events of religious life. Even we religious in an order with its eternal vows tread a road on which God leads and whose corners and end are simply not within our own prescient power. However, hoping and trusting in God's grace, in the 'grace of one's vocation', we summon all our freedom, the execution of which is again a grace, to persevere to the best of our ability on the road we undertook when we entered the order, to be faithful to our vocation, which we should regard with courage and confidence as a part of our divine calling in Jesus to eternal life in God.

4 Being the Church together

The church Christian

A real Christian, one whose Christian life has developed to full maturity, is a church Christian. That means that he lives in a community of Christians extending beyond his own family and including fixed and legitimate institutions going back in due and unbroken succession to the beginning of the Church. For a Catholic Christian those institutions are the Pope and the bishops who live in unity with him.

A particular feature of our times is the existence of a growing number of Christians who want to be Christians without a Church, or to form a kind of new denomination apart from the old denominational Churches. For a number of reasons such an arrangement is impossible in the long run. Firstly, it ignores the fact that the human need for institutionalized community extends to religion; inevitably, therefore, it leads to the atrophy of Christianity in individuals and society. Secondly, Christianity has always existed with an explicit confession of faith, and, following the will of Jesus, has always been the community of the Lord's Supper. Catholic Christians have a sincere love and respect for everyone and everything in which the Spirit of Christ is active outside the Church and in which Jesus's work of freedom and love is continued in the world. At the same time, Catholic Christians are church Christians because they are firmly convinced that this connexion with the Church is also part of the work of Jesus and given to them by his Spirit.

The particular local community existing in legitimate union with the universal Church is itself the Church and not a mere administrative offshoot of a greater Church which uses local establishments to cater for the particular religious needs of individuals and for their individual salvation. The parish is the Church on the spot. The parish has to bring into being the purpose of the Church as such: the appearance of the Holy Spirit of God in freedom and love; the testimony to an everlasting hope for the whole world. It must bring into being the unconditional active love which is only possible when – implicitly or explicitly – people come together in the liberating love of God, in the celebration of Jesus's supper, which makes present his death and resurrection: the tangible signs in our history that God has given himself to us in his own glory to be our salvation. Everything else in the Church (Pope and bishops, clergy and law, organization and the rest) is only a means to the end of creating in the local community and manifesting before the world God and our life in him in freedom, forgiveness and love. Communities and parishes are the Church.

The Church is all of us
The Church, then, is all of us. We are not just objects of pastoral care by an official Church. We are the ones who

are the Church, who have to form and be the Church. The Church is the miraculous family of all those who are with Jesus and in his Spirit. Hence individual Christians cannot start by making demands on a Church which faces them as an external organization. Instead they have to be aware of their mission to join with others, and themselves be the Church. Criticism of the Church is right and necessary, but every critic of the Church must first subject himself to criticism. Is he living up to his responsibility for being the Church with others? Does he live up to it in love, co-operation with others, tolerance, patience, and the realization that he never fully expresses his responsibility for the Church?

The grass-roots Church
The fourth of our introductory theological principles is very important for the present situation. Today every local Church is inevitably, in some degree, a Church of the diaspora. It exists in a profane, secularized society. It is a 'little flock' among the many who are not Christians or regard their baptism and external membership of a religious organization called 'the Church' as an historical and sociological accident which no longer has anything much to do with their real life. The real Christians, those who are not just attached to Christianity as tradition or folklore, live in local Churches in the diaspora, even if the boundaries between the genuinely Christian communities and their secularized surroundings are fluid, unclear and constantly shifting.

To give a theological interpretation of the situation of local Christian Churches in the diaspora would take me too far from my subject. I have room for two points.

31

First, this situation contains a twofold danger. There is the possibility of a liberal sell-out of Christianity through a reduction of its vital religious substance to mere secular humanism, for the sake of good relations with the people surrounding such a small Christian community. The opposite danger is the creation of a ghetto of the 'holy remnant', those who alone are chosen. That makes it easier to withstand the pressure of secularized society and its atheism, and removes the need to bother about others. Unfortunately, it ignores the fact that they too are God's dearly beloved children who, it is to be hoped, by following their consciences also participate in a mysterious way in the Easter mystery of Jesus (as Vatican II emphasized). Both these dangers of our present diaspora situation must be fought. Every Christian, according to his situation and upbringing, is more liable to one or other of these dangers. We must be prepared to let others warn us of any tendency in ourselves to a humanistic reduction of Christianity, or to a narrow, old-fashioned and rigid ghetto mentality.

The fate of the Church will increasingly depend on the continual creation of living grass-roots communities by the initiative of individual Christians. Of course faith and authority come by way of the pope and the bishops to the parish priest from Jesus Christ. In their full extent and competence these ministers are not a democratic institution set up by a group of people who came together to appoint officials for religious purposes defined by the group with its own authority. That is true, but it does nothing to alter the plain fact, which in the present state of society can no longer be ignored, that the actual existence and real effectiveness of the official Church and its office-holders depend increasingly (and crucially) on the people at the bottom. They depend on the good will of the individual Christians who make up a community, and on the responsible collaboration of all the members of that community. In contrast with former centuries, when the official Church relied on the consensus of secular society, today the existence and real efficiency of the Church must be supported by the base, the little flock of firmly believing Christians who make up the Church from below by their faith and faithful lives. If these Christians don't join in or become active, if they don't take up their share of responsibility, the Church ceases to exist, or becomes a mere relic.

Democracy may be a high ideal, and in many things and many areas may be a thoroughly legitimate structural principle in the Church as in other bodies, but it is not the reason why the Church needs the active participation of ordinary Christians. Grass-roots Christians can no longer be a flock willingly led by the clergy.

In a period in which society and Church are no longer co-extensive, in which the state is no longer Christian and public opinion is pluralist, ordinary Christians in the Church acquire a new and inalienable function. However much we may regret and work to prevent the disappearance of a 'national Church' (in so far as one still exists), the Church of the future will be the Church which is constantly reformed from below, and as the Church of those whose own religious conviction makes them join together as the community of Jesus, who was crucified and rose from the dead.

The modern parish

I do not deny the right of individual Christians, according to their particular needs and circumstances, to form, in peace and unity with the Church authorities, grass-roots communities which are not identical with parishes in the traditional sense of the word. On the other hand, in the present situation and for some time to come, parishes too could develop into such living grass-roots communities. Of course there already are good, active parishes which are grass-roots communities of this sort as a result of the dedicated collaboration of priest and people; they are the future of the Church in its present and future diaspora situation in a secularized and pluralistic society.

Some pessimists say that a normal parish can't act as a grass-roots community because the understanding of Christianity and Christian life within it is too diverse to support the common prayer, life and action needed by a genuine grass-roots community. These difficulties certainly exist. They are caused by the difference between progressives and traditionalists, by the pluralism of theologies in people's minds, and so on. And such problems are quite distinct from the difficulties caused by social and cultural differences, which are a greater burden to a traditional parish than when a grass-roots community is formed spontaneously by people with the same attitudes. On the other hand, a grass-roots Christian community formed spontaneously from below also has to overcome difficulties of this second sort; it can't consist merely of socially and culturally homogeneous elements. The same factors should not prevent a parish from being a vital grass-roots community, necessarily composed of Christians with very different religious and theological attitudes. That diversity could be a strength.

But one thing above all should bring such Christians together: their faith in that incomprehensible but liberating mystery which we call God. They share a belief in Jesus Christ as the one through whose life, death and resurrection we have received the irrevocable and historically accessible promise of salvation from this eternal God. They share a desire to love their neighbour without limit in the Spirit of this Jesus, and a desire to live out this faith and love in the one Catholic Church. Where fundamental beliefs of this sort are shared, in spite of any subsequent differences of emphasis or interpretation, there is a basis on which a parish of great cultural and theological diversity can become an active grass-roots community.

Priorities for communities

1. A living community is the Church only where *Christian love truly unites its members*, where each is ready to share the other's burden, where people know each other, help each other, are interested in each other, where there is real co-operation and people can rely on each other. There are in secular society, and in the Church of offices and official institutions, many organizations which offer help to the individual in major and minor crises. Never despise them. The individual Christian has a duty to support them in Christian love and responsibility, and his support for them is part of the exercise of Christian love. But we all know how much

suffering, loneliness and neglect cannot be catered for by such organizations. The responsibility of Christian love for our neighbour cannot be satisfied by the performance of the duties to others which secular society requires of us, whether we like it or not.

This is where the special task of a grass-roots community which is alive in the Spirit and the power of the love of Christ begins. That doesn't mean that only people belonging to an explicitly Christian community are likely to perform the task which official organizations in society and Church can't and shouldn't do for us.

There are, thank God, anonymous Christians, people with open eyes and open hearts for the hidden suffering of their neighbours; for the suffering which can't be removed by the money we give to buy ourselves freedom from our burdensome neighbours. It is the duty of a living Christian community, through its members, individuals and small groups which form to meet the call of love as it makes itself known, to see such suffering and help without a second thought. The suffering may be great or small. It may be lonely old people who cannot be allowed to suffocate in their loneliness. It may require quite ordinary acts of neighbourliness. Perhaps a family has to look after younger children for a few hours so that a mother under stress can finish her housework. Perhaps a father or mother can undertake the private instruction of a child before first communion whose family can't manage sufficient sympathy and help. Perhaps an eye needs to be kept on a neighbour's house to relieve his mind when he goes on holiday. A housewife with a car could take another mum shopping and save time and energy. Once in a while we could give our heart a prod and invite in a neighbour we previously ignored in the security of our concrete barrack-flat. If we did that, we might find a person with a heart and sufferings of his own, sufferings we could help him to bear. We might then discover that our own burden became lighter and that our neighbour was very willing to take some of it from us. And these are quite arbitrary and trivial examples of an important task.

Those are not mere acts of charity between isolated individuals. A living community must be so closely-knit that it becomes a place where the unorganizable can be organized. I must know people who are able and willing to help in situations where I cannot help. I must have the courage and openness to trust them with someone else's suffering. People in a community must know each other. They must get to know each other, talk to each other, consult each other, so that hidden suffering can receive real help. Taken together, a number of small everyday problems and disappointments may be enough to overwhelm an individual and make him bitter or confused. A kind word, friendly attention, a small act of politeness — the sort of thing we take for granted — may make some one else's burden easier to bear.

That isn't obvious 'secular' humanity. Practised consistently, that everyday love is hard and possible only with the power of Jesus, whether given anonymously by the grace of God or explicitly recognized and confessed.

The active love of one's neighbour makes constant calls on the alertness and imagination of a community, but there are many other tasks which involve such a group.

2. A living parish which is really being the Church, and the Church built up from below, should be a *community of prayer*. The Sunday liturgy, following the official liturgy of the Church, should be the centre of a community's prayer life. That liturgy shouldn't be a legalistic interpretation of the Church's liturgical decrees, but the living creation of the community from below. That means participation by the community early on in the preparation of the liturgy. But are there, or should there be, in a living parish or community individual prayer groups 'in between' the official liturgy and private prayer? Why is that sort of thing practically non-existent? What a chore family prayers have generally become, where they still exist. In recent years 'Pentecostal' groups have sprung up within the Catholic Church and won favour with some bishops. They could be more discreet and less exotic, avoiding 'speaking with tongues'. Many more groups of Christians should meet outside official Church auspices to read the scriptures in a variety of experimental forms. They could pray spontaneously; tell each other something about how they pray, and their religious experiences; sing together; even − hardest of all − ask each other uninhibitedly for help and advice. In the past small groups said the rosary together without a priest. Something of that sort, in new and more varied forms allowing scope for individual initiative, are surely possible today.

3. A parish which is alive is the Church on the spot. It has to enjoy a strong and active relationship with the diocese and with the universal Church and its authorities. That is more than giving to the missions. Of course a

living community must be concerned about the mission of the Church in countries where evangelization is in its early stages, but the work of the 'foreign' missions must not be confused with our general duty to help poor nations. I mean more than that: for an individual community, sharing responsibility for the universal Church and for its own diocese is quite compatible with a critical attitude to the Church as it exists, and to its authorities. Such an attitude is a positive part of Church membership. A mature Christian has no right to be a good sheep who accepts the guidance of wise shepherds in silent obedience.

Disputes and opposition, conducted by both sides in faith and love, justice and self-critical caution, are part of the life of the Church. It does no harm for a parish and its priest to disagree, provided that they try to be fair in acknowledging differences on how to be a living Church. Christians must learn that larger differences of opinion exist in the Church. They have to realize that they have the right and the duty to tell the church authorities about the problems and tensions life creates for them. They have the right, through parish councils and similar bodies, to share in making decisions in the Church, and to say where they feel a lack of understanding of their questions and uncertainties, or where they feel let down by statements which are alien to modern attitudes, or by legalistic rules.

Real conflicts and disputes cannot be solved by the exercise of authority. Conflicts arise in any living community; they are part of its life. It's no good using authority to suppress them or declare them non-existent. Yet a part of the community's sharing in the government of the Church is a trust and acceptance of authority, and sympathy and support for office-holders. Sympathy and support are the right not just of the bishop and parish priest, but also of curates and other members of the Church whose main work is to support the life of a parish. In our dealings with such officials we should show patience and a bit of tolerant good-humour and remember that, like the rest of us, they are only limited and sinful humans.

4. *Openness* is another characteristic of a living Christian community, which retains the obligation to preach and (according to its powers) to live, whole and entire, the faith of the Church. In the modern diaspora situation of Christianity the courage for this must be developed by better training. The Church shouldn't try to move with the times by becoming a group with no more than humanitarian or political tendencies and aims. Nor must the Church or individual communities begin a march ghettowards. The Church has to be attractive and invit-ing, even for those whose human and Christian develop-ment has not really reached the point of total identifica-tion with the actual Church, and its institutions and the authority they claim.

The community must be open. Anyone who wants to should have the right to live and work within it. It should be possible to give responsibility within the community to people who, by the standards of strict and in itself legitimate orthodoxy, are not in the full and complete sense Catholic Christians, provided that their aim is not to infiltrate the Church doctrinally or institutionally and change its character. Those who regard themselves as 'progressive' have no reason to despair of the existing Church and to claim bitterly that the hopes of a second spring aroused by Vatican II have withered. Those who call themselves 'conservative' must remember that they have a duty to be charitable, patient and broad-minded towards those about whose orthodoxy they harbour justified or (sometimes) unjustified doubts. The last thing a living community of today can be is a ghetto in which a chosen few live in timid obscurity. It is the community of Pentecost. The Spirit himself has burst open the doors.

5. Ultimately, a living community is supported by an unknown group of Christians who have made the breakthrough into the true freedom of God in faith, hope and love. All Christians are or ought to be on the way to that freedom. There must, however, be some who would never dream of telling themselves and so never dare to tell others, that they have already received the 'baptism of the Spirit' of the radical freedom of love, and who nevertheless live in a community secretly liberated and redeemed by God's grace in the deepest core of their existence. It is those people who ultimately bear the weight of the community and even of its institutions in their real task. Such people can bear a burden without complaining that it belongs to someone else. They can give without thought of a reward. They can return good for evil. They can keep silent when others chatter. They can love when love means more than the natural response to being loved. They can maintain a hopeful and never-failing love of the poor and constantly humiliated Church, which in spite of everything is and remains the

assembly of their brothers and sisters in Jesus. Such people never go astray from the Church. God demands everything of a man, even when he is endlessly patient with him. He demands a man's heart in order to give him himself, the Holy Spirit of freedom, love and the invincible hope of eternal life, which ultimately needs nothing more than God alone.

We must become such people of freedom and love. We shall do so bit by bit, drawing more and more on that centre of our lives which has already been graced by baptism and confirmation. In the jealousy of his love for us, the eternal God is content with no less. The more we become such people, possessed by the liberating Spirit of God, the more we shall build up in our communities the living Church of God and Jesus. Let us be the Church together in patience, in hope and in faith. Let us be the Church in that love which does not pass away.

5 Life in a Christian community

In and *despite* a religious community one has all the experiences no human life is spared: disappointment with oneself; the divide between what one wants to achieve and in fact achieves; familiarity with human weakness and sinfulness (even in a religious community) to which one makes one's own contribution; loneliness felt even in true brotherhood; and so on. The person who can't cope with these things in maturity and courage, and in Christian understanding of community life with Jesus the crucified, can't be helped by a religious community (or any never-to-be-realized utopian community).

If we are to assess religious life as community correctly, we mustn't forget that the finiteness and inadequacies of human life, which we have taken on ourselves with our free determination to live in religion, are, because of this free decision, *more noticeable* than the inadequacies which spring from life unasked and are accepted in silence as part of it all. These adversities are often much greater than the freely-accepted inadequacies of religious life in which a good part of the former can often be avoided. Many religious, however, wish to evade the freely-chosen insufficiencies of religious life

43

by leaving under protest. Then they experience in silence the harsher troubles which come into one's life unbidden. But my insight and experience in other families, groups, social formations, parties, colleges, and so forth, have convinced me that such a religious community of men as that to which I belong has nothing to fear from a comparison with these other groups as regards what is human, fraternal and Christian. In a religious community like ours, the going is sometimes difficult both because an order is out to serve a *cause* (that of Christ and the Church), and because it is not a small circle of people who have nothing but high regard for each other. In the long term, however, only the awareness of having tried again and again to serve a cause selflessly to the best of one's (feeble) ability can bring happiness.

In the Society of Jesus, I found a community with a long history behind it. Such a history, evidently, implies encumbrance, but also, and much more, proven wisdom and richness of experience which no merely theoretical reasoning and planning can replace.

Religious life means the — worthwhile — courage to take advice from others, to conquer an overhasty fondness for one's own opinions and feelings. Once you have dared to try that courage, you notice that entrusting yourself to the larger mind of a group is rewarding.

Today the small individualistic families often waste energy and time unreasonably. A greater co-ordination of such families would often be profitable, even for those who don't want to live in a kibbutz or modern commine. A religious community has, under the guidance of long experience, evolved the sort of life-form that prevents an individual from suffocating in a group. At the same time it gives him the day-to-day advantages of the larger group (especially when it has a number of houses in different places). Anxiety for daily bread and other needs is less for an individual when it is shared ('lay people' should not reproach religious with this, because religious 'pay' for this advantage by sharing a community life, which is not always very easy). The possibility of an individual (and changing) formation of one's own life seems to me to be greater in an order, on the whole, than in 'secular' life where one is mostly 'tied down' to a once-chosen occupation. It is certain, too, that the community life of religious orders normally makes a renunciation of marriage for Christ's sake — which is not to be underestimated — easier and more human.

Yet we can understand religious life as life in community only if we have an inner relationship of unconditional belief in Jesus crucified and risen. Religious life, after all, means serving *him*, continuing *his* life, and witnessing to its power. However, where and when people live this belief and the vocation to bear it witness, there is ultimately no special problem in their coming together in this vocation the better to fulfil *this* mission. The rest follows. We are enriched by such a community only to the extent that we try to give more than to receive.

6 Prayer and the religious

In the language of the Church, people in religious orders are called simply 'religious'. The designation of their state and vocation therefore asserts that they must cultivate their *religio*, their relationship to God, in a special way — 'professionally' one might almost say. That isn't in any way to underestimate the 'laity', because there are many vocations which do not strictly depend on a distribution of the workload in any technical sense but turn a universal human need into an explicitly structural principle of life, even in the everyday sphere.

You have only to think of musicians, poets, politicians, and so on. In those professions an 'amateur' can sometimes make greater progress and a more significant contribution than a professional. If, however, the amateur doesn't try to observe that universal human need, he has 'missed his vocation'. Since the most basic fulfilment of an explicit relationship of man to God is prayer, the latter is an absolutely central part of the religious vocation (even though it is a calling: that is, a grace); it is as central as the universal human and universal Christian elements.

Because grace is given in the free, often wearisome

47

human struggle and does not primarily refer to an emotionally tangible impulse or to relief from responsible exertion, the grace of the call to a religious vocation (which means prayer) is given in the steady and faithful effort of prayer.

To regard the essence of prayer as an old-fashioned and almost mythological form of self-control quite unsuitable for today, as a psychotherapeutic effort at self-possession, as an attempt to attain spiritual calm, as a revision and plan of life, and so forth, is to misunderstand the matter. All those things can result from prayer; but only if they are not the direct object, only if prayer is not regarded as a means of self-perfection; and only if one surrenders selflessly to God in faith, hope and love; ultimately without returning to oneself. The norms that apply to love between people apply to prayer. The former is liberating and satisfying only when the other is really loved and love does not look to its own interests. That a person can actually — and precisely in prayer — lose himself, that the fulfilment of the 'subjectivity' consists and *can* consist precisely in this surrender to the 'objectivity' of God and our neighbour calling us to itself, is a miracle experienced as grace by the person who prays and really loves: the miracle of true freedom.

As I have said, however, that miracle of grace which liberates us in prayer comes about in the steady daily effort to pray, not in the search for subjective experiences that we can enjoy. If this is rightly understood and appreciated, it is clear that prayer has a deep inner unity and a relationship of mutual conditioning with selfless love, with that, therefore, which from a negative angle is characterized in tradition and also in biblical language as 'self-denial', 'renunciation', and so on.

The person who truly forgets himself (because he is absorbed in God and his neighbour, in God in unrewarded service of man) can pray, already prays, and in order to pray needs only let the process of his self-forgetfulness with all its implications begin. From this point of view, the 'horizontalism' so much prized today is useful *provided that* it is rightly understood to imply no absolute opposition to 'verticalism' (rightly understood), that this verticalism is not misconstrued as the enjoyment of religious 'interiority' taken to mean a dispensation from selfless service of one's neighbour or compensation for the 'frustration' of unrewarded service.

It does not follow from this that the strain on man from the demands of a vocation today, of activity today, must necessarily mean endangering or reducing prayer. When this activity is in the service of power, self-assertion, ambition, and so on, evidently it becomes a danger and an obstacle to prayer, just as self-indulging introversion (as I said earlier) is the ruin of true prayer. However, if a person really serves his neighbour in selflessness and thanklessness and is also reverently attentive that his service is performed even when it brings no tangible satisfaction, he certainly learns to pray.

Not every really selfless person, perhaps, knows that he is already actually praying; that is, freely surrendering to that unutterable mystery which alone (unlike finite man who can never justify such love on his own) can receive such self-surrender. We Christians, however, can and should know that we can expressly pray when our prayer is the self-awareness of selfless love (for God in man). As Christians we should know that when we pray in that way, we are praying explicitly with the Son who in the darkness of death, out of love for his brothers, humbly surrendered to the mystery he called his Father.

7 Obedience and freedom

This chapter was written with a primarily apostolic community in mind; basically, however, it deals with religious obedience in general. Even though in the first place obedience (and the office of the superior) is understood functionally, in certain circumstances the relation of a superior to his subordinates can be that of a 'spiritual father', or one 'animated by the Spirit' (*pneumatikos*), as in monasticism. Where that is exemplified in the person of the superior, it is to be welcomed. There is an unbroken tradition to that effect, in ancient monasticism and in Ignatius of Loyola. But it can't rightly be demanded and standardized (even though that happened for many years). And it can't be expected in every case without destroying the proper essence of religious obedience.

The question of knowing God's will in the here-and-now, and therefore of obedience to *God*, as far as the individual and the community are concerned, is not expressly posed here. Instead, I deal with the relation between superior and subordinate: with religious obedience in the strict sense.

1. It doesn't matter if obedience in the religious

community is slightly demythologized in the theory of ascetic literature and the practice (perhaps we should call it 'preconciliar') of religious life.

(*a*) Religious obedience (with which the present reflexions deal exclusively, because the general problem of authority and freedom, obedience in the family, civil society and the Church cannot be considered here, although much that is important for religious obedience would arise from such consideration) has *in itself* nothing to do with the relation between the disciple and his master, guru, 'spiritual father', father confessor, and so forth. If there are traces of that confusion between 'religious superior' and 'spiritual father' in the Rules of religious orders or in a widespread ascetically justified practice, and correspondingly in the behaviour of religious towards superiors understood in this way, they should be suppressed. Then one can start afresh thinking through a correct theory and praxis of 'accounting in conscience' to the religious superior.

A clear delineation between religious superior (in the social areas of a religious order) and a 'spiritual father' (or friend in the confidential, private sphere) does not, of course, mean that superiors and subjects should or could meet only in the area of properly legal regulations.[1]

(*b*) The religious superior is not 'God's representative' in that he could claim or expect, by reason of his office alone, a special 'inspiration', 'enlightenment' or particular dispensation of providence from God. There is no special presumption in favour of the correctness or suitability of his orders in practice merely because they come from him as a religious superior; there is a presumption that they should be followed, because and in so far as they are orders of a legitimate social authority.

The superior *is* 'God's representative' in that he is the concrete bearer of a legitimate (and therefore ultimately divinely willed) administrative competence in a society which itself, because it is meaningful, may be regarded as God-willed. One may urge that this society in our case is *ultimately* the *Church* (and not a profane society) and therefore claim an ecclesiological, to some extent 'pneumatic' quality for such an authority in an order, but since no individual religious order is identical with the Church (despite all the Church's approval of it), one must beware of appropriating excessively lofty prerogatives to the authority of the religious superior at the expense of other legitimate authorities. That is not to deny that the specific meaning of authority in an order derives from the significance and aim of an ecclesially approved religious community as part of the Church (not necessarily, of course, in a local sense).

(*c*) Religious obedience should not, therefore, be falsely and superfluously underpinned by paternalistic ideologies. Religious are not children. Their obedience as such has nothing to do with the obedience of minors living with their parents at home. A religious superior has much to learn from a father and his association with his grown-up sons, but he is not a 'father'. One may draw comparisons between a father and a superior, and tradition has done so with no little acumen and thoughtfulness; but such analogies today are more likely to hamper than help matters.

2. Religious obedience is primarily to be viewed from the point of view of its *functional* significance in a society which has a common work and a common aim.

(*a*) An order is a society and therefore has a job to do and a purpose in mind to which all its members must contribute. This is true especially of an apostolic community[2] in which the specific aim of the order as a society is not identical with the spiritual-subjective aim of the individual (personal salvation).[3] Such a society must necessarily distinguish the social ('political') sphere (in which, in part at least, a certain conformity is rightly demanded) and the private sphere of its members.

(*b*) Religious obedience means the moral (freely undertaken) obligation on the part of the members of the order to follow the directives issued in the public sector by the superiors (in accordance with the order's Rule) for the attainment of the order's purpose. It is quite indifferent (cf. under 4 below) how the appointment of the authority and the manner in which the material content of an instruction is decided on are to be correctly regulated in a particular society.

Instructions[4] which originate from the society in question,[5] which are represented and issued by particular individual agents legitimately appointed for that purpose and which lay an obligation on the individual even though he has not yet of himself made the content of the instruction a norm of his conduct, are necessarily part of any society. This is because (leaving other reasons aside here) the process of reflexion on the material justice of the content of the command (despite its necessity and moral obligation) can never *adequately* in finite time and with finite means be taken to an ultimate conclusion; therefore in every decision a moment of free decision (which cannot be adequately reflected upon) supervenes on the process of purely rational argumentation, a moment which, whether posited by a collectivity or by an individual, is in any case not always posited by the one whom the decision obliges to observance.

(*c*) Obedience, then, in its proper essence (without prejudice to what is to be said under 3), is functional: it exists to integrate and co-ordinate the activities of the individual members of the religious order to its one, common (apostolic) aim. In so far as and to the extent that this common mission is supported by the common life of the order's members as a presupposition of their common (apostolic) mission and work, obedience naturally applies to the regulation of the common life. That is true, however, *only* to the extent that a certain moderation and a certain manner of common life as a precondition and means of the common (apostolic) mission are laid down in the Rule and practice of the order.

(*d*) It follows that the superior's competence of command is strictly limited by the objective suitability (functional justness) of the content of the command for the (apostolic) aims of the order. The superior, therefore, has the moral and legal obligation to command only what serves, and circumstances permitting better serves, these aims. Where such a functional appropriateness is lacking, obedience *in itself* ceases. Where the

command in its material content *contravenes* the
order's purpose and (apostolic) mission unequivocally
and without any doubt and in clear defiance of the
presumption in favour of the command of the legitimate
superior, even though one cannot prove that the command in its content contravenes the *moral* law and
that one would on *that* score (cf. 6 below) be entitled
to refuse obedience, the subject is not bound by it. –
It follows from this functional essence of authority
(superior) and obedience (subordinate) that the relation imples no superiority and subordination in the
personal field.

Superior and subject are *both* subordinate to the
common cause and in its one service have only a different function. The function of bringing to a conclusion
in finite time the reflexion – which is ultimately borne
by all but can never be adequately exercised by all – on
the decision demanded by the cause (the order's mission) and so of articulating the cause's actual imperative
(in so far as it can be known here and now) is the
proper, 'inevitable' business of the superior, but it does
not imply any subordination of the 'subject' in the
personal sphere. Religious orders must evolve a style of
communication between superior and 'subject' which
takes this into account.

It is not the purpose of commands to 'advance the
individual in virtue', to 'mortify' him, to 'humble' him,
and so on. Of course this does not mean that in the case
of any given command the subject has the right and
duty to obey only when he himself has *positively*
appreciated its functional expedience by making his
own judgment. Such a requirement would be

equivalent to denying the need for an authority in the society (cf 2b) or in other words to postulating that formal and material authority are always and in every case identical.

(*e*) This functional essence of authority and obedience in a religious order evidently does not imply that the *actual* relationship between superiors and subordinates is governed *solely* by this bald (almost legal) principle. Because it must be realized by *actual* people, many human virtues are involved: sobriety, impartiality, patience, courtesy, fellowship, broad-mindedness, humour, and so on.

3. Even on this understanding of obedience, the Christian-spiritual essence of obedience (as an evangelical counsel and the discipleship of Christ) can be completely observed.

(*a*) First of all, in our actual life-situation and present ('infralapsarian') economy of salvation, there are conflict situations between the 'needs' of a society and those of the individual, between the abilities of the individual and the external possibilities of their satisfaction, between directly perceptible 'happiness' and moral 'duty', and so forth, which cannot be entirely avoided. Acceptance of such a (here and now) insuperable situation belongs to the human and Christian living-out of existence, to its 'cross' (like physical pain, illness, death, and so on) which must be borne as an act of hoping faith.

A Christian, who knows that he will meet this 'cross' situation in his life at some time or other and that its acceptance in faith and hope out of love for God and his incomprehensible decrees is the decisive act of his life, has the courage to face this cross situation actively and not merely wait for it passively, so that he can exercise his hoping faith. This is the meaning of voluntary Christian 'resignation'[6] which can be exercised in the different dimensions of human life. Voluntary 'resignation' is as it were a dress rehearsal for the believing, hoping acceptance of *the* resignation which — as death — every individual is inescapably called on to exercise. The person who lives this active readiness for Christ's cross (even though that cross is unpredictable) realizes the conduct which the 'evangelical counsels' are designed to foster and which finds its concrete form in them.

(*b*) In the reality of human life, the actual commands of the authority in a society (even though it is purely 'functional' in the service of this society's overriding aim or at least only this intention is consciously at work) can lead to the conflict situations, 'cross' situations, mentioned in 3a. The superior *intends* no such conflict situation and may not do so, but in actual fact such situations do often arise: they are unavoidable in practice.

The work demanded in the concrete by the aim and mission of a religious order will not be achieved without friction and will not always accord with what the subject *directly* experiences as his inclinations, as the satisfaction of his wishes and needs, even when he basically approves of the order's aim and mission and makes them his own. Only the person who would deny what was said under 3a as true of human life in general could maintain that a command is always illegitimate if it contradicts the directly experienced inclination of the subordinate and is therefore felt to 'frustrate' or 'prejudice' the development of his personality. If this were so, no authority at all would be needed to terminate the decision-making process in the concrete (cf. 2b).

(c) Anyone who binds himself to obedience in an order freely exposes himself to a possible new cross situation, even though the manufacture of such a situation is not the purpose of obedience or of authority with its functional essence. He binds himself to an evangelical counsel. He states his readiness not only to accept an eventual situation (created by a superior's command) of 'frustration', of 'damage' to the fulfilment of his empirically immediate striving for happiness as a permanently unavoidable factor (because no such situation is entirely avoidable in any social co-existence in which conflicts of interest can never be entirely removed without loss) but also positively to accept it in the sense of the evangelical counsel as an act of faith and hope. He freely and with his eyes open runs the 'risk' of the cross given by obedience which is thoroughly intelligible as a rational (that is, 'functional') activity.

(d) It must again be stressed that this 'risk' for someone who binds himself to obedience can be intended as a situation of his faith and hope beyond what is perceivable 'in this world' and should be intended in *religious* obedience, but that the superior may intend to command only what is appropriate, that is, something which, as far as can be ascertained, serves the society's

59

mission and purpose.

(*e*) The observance of a command issued by the religious superior is normally conducive to the development of the subject's personality in activating its possibilities and talents (and therefore to 'earthly' happiness too) in the sense and manner in which the order's aim and work further the individual's personality and are therefore satisfying to him. (A precondition of this satisfaction in obedience is naturally the genuine, undivided and permanent 'realization' of the meaningfulness of the order's aims.) But just as the pursuit of other goals and missions, equally meaningful in an innerworldly context, can lead to 'tragic' situations (the doctor is infected; the politician is shot; the marriage partner becomes incurably ill; a school lesson miscarries; a research project comes to nothing; senility destroys a life's ambition; and so forth), so religious obedience (unintentionally from the superior's point of view, but inevitably in the concrete) leads to similar frustrating situations which must be accepted.

The 'heathen' will silently *try* to bear such situations, which crop up in everyone's life; the Christian, and particularly the Christian who is a religious, will gladly take them on himself, and with them the 'frustrations' which obedience can entail, as the self-extension of death throughout life, of the death, that is, which he has determined to undergo with the crucified Lord as an act of belief in eternal life. In this sense, and only in this sense, he accepts the renunciation which obedience can involve. There is no 'masochistic' search for humiliation here, no craving for 'submissiveness', no fear of one's own responsibility, no morbid appetite for death, but on the one hand a sober understanding (3b above) that the achievement of a common goal requires the concrete coordination of wills and activities which entails what are called authority, commands, obedience in a society, and on the other (3c) the understanding that in practice obedience can lead to situations which are cross situations from which no life is free. The religious has only to declare himself prepared to accept this obedience in freedom to welcome the cross in a *Christian* way.

(*f*) The religious therefore does not properly abdicate the freedom which is an essential and inalienable property of human existence. First of all , it must be seen that every use of freedom is also, existentially and in society inevitably, the acceptance of restrictions and constraints.

The free assumption of religious life is no exception to this, and therefore needs no special justification. Every act of freedom is always at the same time the rejection of another possibility which could also have been realized, and creates objective situations which have their own legality — which also narrows freedom.

The religious community and the superior's orders must also leave the religious a wide field in which he may exercise his own power of decision in his life and activity and in which his freedom cannot and should not be limited by commands.

The more the subordinates are associated in establishing the material justice of the command — this positively respects the essence of obedience as a functional necessity in a community and means no 'dilution' of obedience — the less will it appear that obedience restricts the freedom and responsibility of the subordinate. — The latter does not 'sacrifice' his freedom. The false mythologization of religious obedience must vanish from ascetic literature. The religious does not 'sacrifice' his freedom any more than anybody else who (in getting married, in professional responsibilities, and so on) exposes himself, for the genuine realization of his freedom, to the commitments entailed by the freely chosen cause.

4. The concrete shape of religious obedience is variable and dependent on many historically changing social, psychological and many other conditions. This variability, historical and therefore open to the future, can be faced without embarrassment.

(a) The proper *essence* of a superior's command and of obedience is not lost when the concrete bearer of authority, the method of establishing the material content of a concrete command, the extent of objects of possible commands alter and indeed perhaps *must* alter to suit the social situations. So, for example, without affecting the substance of obedience, the *bearer* of a decision can be a single person *or* a collectivity, government can be 'monarchical' *or* 'democratic': in neither case is the author of the imperative identical with the one to whom the imperative is addressed. The essence of obedience therefore remains unaffected by this distinction.

The question of which precise *method* of decision-making is preferable (a question ultimately to be decided on the aims of the community) must depend on the probably greater efficiency of the various possible decision-making processes as well as, in many cases, on historical tradition. The importance of this question should not be over-estimated, because the method generally depends on the concrete *application* of the 'constitution' of a religious order, which cannot usually be *legally* enforced and controlled unequivocally, more than on the constitution itself, which can never be such that abuses are impossible. – Similarly it is not incompatible with the essence of obedience that the material *content* of a command is established in cooperation with a number of people (advisers), according to specific rules of procedure, and so on.

When (for example, by decree of a general chapter) the members of such a council have a deciding vote, the circles of those who command and those who obey partially overlap. This makes no difference to the essence of the obligation to obedience in so far as it affects an individual inside or outside the circle of 'those who give the orders'. Similarly a democratic (collective) method of reaching a decision at the *lowest* level (that of the particular instruction to a particular individual) is still quite compatible with the essence of obedience. Whether something would be expedient in this case or could be enforced without bureaucratic formalities is naturally another question, which could quite possible by answered in the negative. – Likewise the *extent* of the content of a command is conditioned by historical and social factors. Not everything that was once the object of a superior's competence must necessarily remain so for ever. (I am thinking of the censuring of correspondence, the 'need to follow one's conscience', and so on.)

(*b*) In consequence, changes in its actual form, whether they be slow or rapid, unreflexive or reflexive, belong to the concrete (and therefore always historical) essence of obedience. Therefore it cannot be the superior's function to wish to use the power he has 'now' to prevent such changes always and in every case.

5. The problem of the *vow* of obedience as one of the evangelical counsels is not to be treated here because the theology and problematics of *all* religious vows would have to be considered *ex professo*. The fundamental question would be whether the vow applies directly to the vowed object itself, on the unexpressed assumption that the (lifelong) attainment of the virtue vowed is *always* possible providing that it is freely willed, because its other preconditions are definitely and always present, or whether it applies to the cbject only on the hypothesis that the other conditions of observance (of the virtue), which are independent of the person's freedom and which certainly cannot always be presumed to be present, will prove in the course of life to be present in fact.

To put it another way, does a person directly vow the lifelong observance of the virtue concerned *or* the *free* control of his life and the development of his personality in such a way that he can attain (and also attains) the observance of the vowed virtue *if* the partial causes of life's course and personality development withdrawn from the control of one's personal freedom do not make

the attainment of observance impossible? As I mentioned, however, I am not going to deal with this question in any more detail here.

6. Superiors and subordinates must reckon with a
legitimate reservation or protest in conscience which
from the subordinate's point of view would mean that
he could not in conscience obey the command.[7]

(a) If Vatican II admits without reservation that even an
atheist may be an atheist in good faith, it cannot be
contested that a superior as well as a subordinate can
make a mistake on the moral quality of a command
with an erroneous judgment that cannot here and now
be rectified even with goodwill. This is even truer today,
when life is so much more complex and less penetrable
than before, and it cannot therefore be expected that
for every single case patterns of conduct traditionally
tested and morally weighed, about whose positively
moral quality there can be no serious doubt, will be
readily available.

(b) Under certain circumstances, then, a superior can
issue, in perfectly good faith, a command which is
objectively immoral. In inculpable and invincible error,
the subordinate can judge that a command, although
good, is morally objectionable and therefore not to be
followed. Basically every command is subject to the
moral judgment of the subordinate. The latter cannot
waive his duty to ask and judge whether *his* actions,
for which he is himself inalienably responsible, are
morally justified or not. This judgment on *his own*
actions, however, cannot be passed without judgment

65

on the moral quality of the command. In making this latter judgment, he may presume the superior's competence, good faith, and so on, and may also certainly presume the moral legitimacy of the command. He is not thereby, however, dispensed from the duty of making his own judgment, and the presumption is no more than a presumption which can be suspended by a − real or imaginary − sounder insight.

(c) When a subordinate declares that after careful consideration he cannot obey a superior's particular command because he regards it as immoral, the superior should proceed in the following way:

(i) Circumstances permitting, he must inform the subordinate that not everything which seems and is judged to be less expedient, less favourable to personality development, and so on, is, on that score alone, immoral. If this were so, no decision or command would ever be made, because the content of any command can always be contrasted with another content even more expedient, more favourable to personality development, and so forth.

(ii) If an objection of conscience is not cleared up by an unbiased discussion in mutual respect and love (the superior, for example, withdraws his command as objectively immoral, or the subordinate understands that his conscience was ill-informed), the superior should (1) if it is a matter of little significance concerning this individual alone, out of respect for the subordinate's conscience give way, not insist on his command to *this* subordinate, but take suitable steps to ensure that the matter of the command is carried out by others who do not have an objection in conscience. This course of action seems to suggest itself because one may never force a person into something which is against his conscience and even if nothing else is commanded on other grounds, no one should suffer because he follows his conscience. *If*, on the other hand, (2) the conscientious objection leads the subordinate to refuse such measures as the superior, after mature verification, considers to be constitutive of or indispensable and necessary to the order and its life, the superior can suggest to the subordinate, if he stands by his conscientious objection, that he ask to leave the order or (if the request is not made) simply dismiss him from the order. No one may be forced into actions which are against his conscience; but the conscientious objector has no right to force the order, by his objection, into an action or toleration which the order regards as a contradiction of its substance. (For example, nobody can, by appealing to his conscience, wish to be an atheist or a heretic or married *and* a religious.) *Every* (ecclesial or secular) society basically claims the right to take action against even 'conscientious' objectors in certain circumstances.[8]

Notes

[1] Superior and subordinate are human beings, Christians, housemates, serving a common aim. It is evident, therefore, that there are a great many relationships given and offered which codetermine the *joint* relationship of one to the other. Here, however, the object of any reflexions is the essence of religious obedience as such, and I am therefore not obliged to consider all the other relations that may obtain at the same time.

67

2 To gain a clearer insight into the functional quality of religious obedience, I am reflecting here and in what follows primarily on orders with an 'apostolic' purpose. If and in so far as there should be *purely* 'contemplative' orders, and on that point it is more than just a question of shifts in emphasis, however important they may be, there would be in a contemplative community a particular life-style and a permanent Rule of contemplative life (but which should be constantly under review if temporal changes demand it), and the superior in such an order would then, on the strength of his right to claim a subordinate's obedience, have only the duty to watch over the observance and concretization of this permanent Rule. This is not to contest the right of a contemplative order to aspire to a synthesis between a superior in this sense and a 'spiritual father' of the kind envisaged of the abbot in St Benedict's Rule (for example). The question then is only how far the constant search for a superior who can also be the 'father' of his monks is successful in reality.

3 This distinction, which enables the subsequent distinction between the private and social dimensions of the religious to be drawn, was clearly made as long ago as Suarez, *De religione Societatis Jesu*, Bk. I, chap. 2, where the author offers important considerations on this point which hold true even if we discount Suarez's 'triumphalism' with regard to the Jesuits.

4 I do not use the concept 'instruction' here in the narrow, specific sense we give the word elsewhere to distinguish a proper command from what is not more than an 'instruction'. Cf. for example, 'On the theological problems entailed in a "Pastoral Constitution" ', in my *Theological Investigations*, 10, 293-317.

5 This is the correct formulation, firstly because all superiors even in an order are supported by the meaning and legitimacy of the community itself: *they* serve *it*, not *vice versa*; secondly, all superiors are directly or indirectly elected; finally, all commands must remain within the scope of the order's constitution. It is therefore quite correct to say that a superior's commands are instructions originating from the community itself and borne by the community.

6   On this, cf. 'Reflections on the Theology of Renunciation' and 'The Passion and Ascetism', *Theological Investigations*, 3, 47-85.

7   On this, cf. 'Christ as the example of priestly obedience', *Servants of the Lord* (London, 1964). On a Christian view of conscientious objection, it must be seen that it is not only a lapse, perhaps often unavoidable but none the less regrettable, in the functioning of command and obedience, but also an event absolutely central in the life of Christ in his conflict with the politico-religious authorities, which he basically acknowledges, and therefore the Christian should not be surprised when something similar happens in the Church and the religious life.

8   Cf. for example, 'The Theology of Power', *Theological Investigations*, 4, 391-409, and 'The Dignity and Freedom of Man', *ibid.*, 2, 235-263.

8 Enthusiasm and the religious

There can be few religious today who are unaware of the movements covered by the terms 'enthusiastic', and 'charismatic'. They are groups committed to living and working within the Catholic Church but at the same time regarding themselves as the recipients of a charismatic experience of the Spirit. The tendency originated in Catholic universities in the United States. It takes many forms. They are as diverse as the experiences enjoyed (or at least claimed as having been enjoyed) at meetings. These are prayer meetings with singing, scripture readings and interpretation, and reports of individual religious experience. There are experiences of a liberation by the Spirit in joy, peace and love; testimonies to experiences of the presence of Christ and baptism with the Spirit understood as radical rebirth through surrender to Jesus; and charisms of prophecy, healing and speaking with tongues as well as interpretations of such utterances.

The few principles (mainly dogmatic) I give here are intended to help religious to confront the charismatic movement sympathetically and yet critically. Of their nature, such theological principles must remain very general. They have to be tested against the particular shape of a charismatic prayer-group, and adapted as necessary.

1. Experience of the Spirit is met with. The existence and possibility of spiritual experience which is rightly regarded as the effect of God's grace is attested to by Scripture and the experience of devout Christians in all ages. Spiritual experience of this kind is not limited to the reception of the sacraments or private prayer. According to Scripture it can occur where a group is gathered together for prayer and individuals break through the barriers of their private religious existence, and gain courage to testify or pray with and for each other. It can occur where common prayer is not just the performance — however seriously intended — of a fixed liturgy but a spontaneous creation, in which worshippers give one another the strength to respond freely to the presence of the Lord. The experience of the Spirit means freedom to laugh, cry, sing and clap one's hands; and the courage to speak from the heart a word of instruction or comfort.

2. Nevertheless, even when regarded as grace, charism, and the working of the Holy Spirit, all such spiritual experience occurs only as something which is already ours. It is always subject to the laws of human psychology, a person's character, previous experience and theological knowledge (including errors). There are no purely divine experiences of grace; there are only 'incarnate' spiritual experiences. In his experience of the breath of the Spirit, even the most charismatically inspired person and Christian *also* finds himself. This is

why it is no surprise, and also no proof that a religious experience is not the work of the Spirit, that at least on occasion very similar religious experiences occur in the most diverse Christian churches and generally outside Christianity. Experiences which even devout Christians interpret as typical experiences of grace sometimes occur in an apparently totally secular form among non-Christians. One example is the feeling of a sudden release from depression and apathy into freedom and power.

It is also clear why all those experiences which we regard as the work of the Spirit and of grace require the 'distinguishing of spirits'. Not everything which derives its urgency from an emotion which seems to overwhelm a person's whole energy or presents itself as a completely unexpected insight and experience; not every experience which overpowers and overwhelms with its newness a person's self (as he has previously known it), is for that reason the pure action of God's Spirit. The various layers of a human being contain much more than he has been made aware of through previous environmental experience. A new experience of this sort, which he finds totally novel, does not necessarily come from God or the devil. It can be the revelation of things which are part of a man but which hitherto were inaccessible to him. The experience of belonging to an enthusiastic prayer group may have opened the door. 'Distinguishing spirits' is necessary, and for this task even a prayer group of this kind must be guided by the orthodox doctrine of the Church and the traditional criteria for such cases laid down in the spiritual teaching of the past. Sober reason and the traditions of an order have their place too, relative though they may be.

3. It is not easy to determine more precisely what part of such incarnate grace comes from God and what from human nature. It is hard to set up criteria, either for a particular case or as general principles. The distinguishing of spirits I mentioned earlier does not, strictly, relate to the problem I am dealing with now. What was involved there was distinguishing, in such 'religious' experiences and impulses, between what is genuinely salutary and God-given on the one hand and what only seems the work of grace and ultimately in fact leads people astray. The present problem is much less important, since even the 'purely human' can rightly be regarded as the grace of God. Someone may derive pleasure from a good impulse. Someone else may greet his neighbour with genuine openheartedness. A person, for whatever reason or by whatever means, may suddenly be lifted out of a depressive phase into a joyful, or at least brave involvement with life. Another may hear the words of the Gospel with new ears, as though he had never heard them before. Someone else may acquire the patience to come to terms with himself and his limitations. It is right and proper for all these people to celebrate these hopes and achievements as the grace of God. They do not need to work out exactly what happened since all good and all enlightenment always come to us ultimately from the bounty God lavishes on us. The most ordinary things which contribute to salvation can be regarded as God's grace, and the most extraordinary charisms are still human.

To determine what is human and what divine in an

enthusiastic experience, the following suggestions may be helpful. Any aspect of a religious experience must be the action of grace and the work of God if it silently and unobtrusively delivers a person up in total hope and love to the inexpressible mystery we call God. (There may not necessarily be such an element.) It must not be contemplation or search for some particular element of religious awareness, but the presence of the totality of that awareness which no longer has a single 'name', the unnameable mystery of God, the only true salvation. In a Christian, this consciousness through grace of the nearness of the God who gives himself to us is explicitly Christian because it is aware that its strength and possibility derive from Jesus's unconditional surrender of himself in death to the Father through the Holy Spirit. All individual elements of the religious sense (individual theological concepts, particular religious and moral goals, particular commitments, and so forth) can be regarded with some probability as God-given and the work of grace if they do not deflect but intensify this restless openness to God. A further condition is that they satisfy the criteria for the distinguishing of spirits outlined above.

I have dealt with principles which are necessarily abstract, and much more could be said about particular phenomena which occur in these enthusiastic prayer meetings. But my purpose here has been to encourage religious communities to meet such enthusiastic movements with critical sympathy. They can learn something from them, even if only the rediscovery of their own past. It would be wrong to treat every fashionable breeze as the breath of the Spirit, but the Spirit will breathe today in the Church and in religious orders in the forms he chooses. If in the process he breaks down some theological rationalism, some inhuman worship of regulations, some soulless ritual and in its place sets joy, peace and trust, that can only be a blessing for religious orders.

9 The challenge of growing old

Old age is a special challenge in the Christian life. If that life is to be furthered and lived by religious in ways and in institutions which are expressly directed towards it, then religious orders must make the Christian fulfilment of old age their business.

Human life, which is governed by what is human and therefore by what is Christian, is not a series of periods differing only in their biological and physiological characteristics. The biological difference, which is easy to see, permeates man in *all* his dimensions. In more profound philosophical and theological terms, this connexion could also be seen the other way round: because man as a free temporal spirit has a history, he has a period of maturity and termination in a personal old age, and therefore a biological substratum which corresponds to that old age (which is primitively and positively intended) and makes it possible.

Old age has special characteristics (which are both privilege and burden) not given in any other period of life. Wisdom literature pointed out a long time ago that a person can be mature and fulfilled many years before his time. But if one is to understand such an optimistic assertion (as a general observation) about a young person who is young psychologically and not only in years (in rapid inner age), such an assertion, strictly speaking, can only laud the fact that so fortunate a youth has filled and exhausted his period of life in an exemplary fashion. But it cannot seriously maintain that he has reaped in his early years, on the battlefield of his life, what one can actually sow and harvest only on the field of old age.

Old age is a grace (= both mission and risk) not given to everyone, just as, in the Christian understanding, there are other possibilities and situations reckoned as graces which are granted to some and withheld from others. That must be seen and accepted as part of 'God's will'. In this connexion we should not take facile comfort in the ultimately erroneous thought that old age, like many other life situations, is a merely external situation which does not terminate in the definitive sequel of life but is merely like a costume in which a person plays a rôle in the theatre of life which remains extraneous to himself, which he simply drops at death, which does not – even transformed – end in the personal definitiveness we call eternal life. Such an opinion (only superficially pious) does not take man's history really seriously: 'eternity' is the (transformed) definitiveness of history itself. Whether a person dies young or dies old, he takes this temporal destiny of his into his definitiveness as an inner moment of it.

Therefore growing old is a really serious matter. It is a grace, a mission and the risk of radical failure. It is a part of human and Christian life which (like every other part of life) has its insubstituable and irreplaceable importance. That is particularly true since old age must be understood not simply as life's running out but as life's 'coming to definitiveness', even when that happens under the paralyzing influence of slow, biological death. *Mutatis mutandis*, the same thing may be said of old age as is said of death in its Christian understanding. We undergo death not in medical cessation but in the length and breadth of life, with all its different phases.

In earlier times, human societies (from primitive to highly developed cultures) awarded old age *institutionally* a particular role distinct from other people's. They acknowledged, *at the social level*, the human and Christian uniqueness of senescence. For example, there was a council of wise elders, a minimum age for admission to high office, social customs which respected older people, a place of honour, a special dress, the council of elders as bearers of tradition, of law, of the administration of justice and of the control of 'resources', and so on. Today experience and the passing on of experience are not so unequivocally tied to old people, and the latter often find themselves pushed rather to one side as inmates of old folks' homes. There is talk of the elderly as burdens on society. An age limit is set for certain social positions (even the cardinals' right to vote for a pope). Yet, conversely, groups of old people can form something like 'pressure groups' in politics, either through their own efforts or simply because of a top-heavy structure of the age pyramid, and we revolt against that. Ultimately it is simply that much has been changed in society and its relation to the elderly by the fact that proportionally there are many more old people in the population than before, their numbers have risen, their rarity value has dropped. Their function in society

79

can't be the same as in the past.

All that has an effect on the elderly members of religious orders, especially because in orders, apart from the universal reasons for change, the age pyramid has changed unfavourably because of a considerable shrinkage in recruitment. It will change even more in the future.

If the orders are to live human and Christian life and salvation in Christ exemplarily and convincingly, elderly religious and the orders themselves have the duty of living old age in a Christian way and of creating the necessary institutional preconditions for that. The number of questions this raises is almost incalculable. They can certainly often be answered by a healthy life-instinct and unreflecting daily experience, but it is not always so easy.

How does the age pyramid in a religious society today differ from in the past? What will it be like in a few years' time? What human and economic requirements arise from this today? How will the elderly be treated in religious orders? Will there be special homes for them? Will they be shunted off into sidings? Or will the orders enable their elderly members to lead a Christian and human life in peace, joy and security? Have the orders already given thought to the proper participation of their elderly members in the leadership of the community? Is the leadership superannuated? Is there in the community the courage and the tradition to relinquish an office opportunely in favour of younger members? Are there legal rulings for this? Will they be drawn up? Will appropriate canonical regulations deal with periodical change in offices so that the same group of older members stays at the helm? Regardless of the principle (opportune for today) that middle age should according to the Rule occupy the decisive offices in a religious community (because of the accelerated speed of change in all societies, the career situation which accompanies an office today, and so forth), is there an (eventually institutionalizable) possibility of letting the experience of the old as such be heard? Do the orders consider how it feels to be pensioned off as superfluous and a burden on the society? (A merely verbal declaration is no good here.)

Will all possibilities to offer elderly members other work to replace the work they can no longer manage, be exhausted? Are there no cases in which elderly nuns are still set to unworthy drudgery because the orders lack the spirit to temper the work to their present strength? Does one really learn in the orders to bear with dignity the burden and disillusionment of old age? Are there 'embittered' old folk even in religious orders? Why? What should be done to be in time to prevent this state of affairs? Are anniversaries (jubilees of profession and so on) celebrated in a purely routine fashion (or perhaps not celebrated at all), or is the community's heart and love in it? Couldn't some elderly nuns become something like 'spiritual directors' for other nuns, in the wise detachment of their old age?

Is it conceivable to introduce differences in the regulation of a religious house which would take the needs of the older members more into account without having to snatch at 'dispensations' by way of accommodating the Rule? Are there peculiarities in the traditional attitudes of mothers superior who are perhaps still acceptable to

81

the younger members but certainly not to the nuns who are older than the mothers superior themselves? Do nuns, who are qualified for it, have also the courage to remind an elderly colleague of the human and Christian task of their old age when one sees that in false struggle for power or in embitterment or otherwise she will not face up to the new opportunities of old age, or does one say simply: there is nothing to be done here, let her go her own way?

Such questions, recorded here quite unsystematically, could be multiplied without difficulty. They were intended simply to give a slightly more concrete form to the statement with which I started: old age is a new Christian challenge in life and therefore sets orders and their superiors new and special challenges with regard to those who are permitted, by God's grace, to live out their old age in religion.

Questions on the care of elderly colleagues

1. Do you have special celebrations for birthdays, name-days and jubilees, and do you give the person concerned sufficient say in the celebrations?

2. Do you concern yourself with the old people on days which are *not* feastdays? Or are feastdays only the appeasement of a guilty conscience?

3. Do you bear with repeated accounts of events, stories and jokes long since familiar to all?

4. Do you respect the conservative element in the overall attitude of elderly colleagues?

5. Do you know what you can give an elderly colleague to afford him pleasure? A book? a box of chocolates? a record?

6. Do you point out to elderly colleagues films or television programmes likely to interest them?

7. Do you occasionally submit your own affairs to an elderly fellow-religious for his opinion?

8. Do you ask him for advice, or is his 'chatter' unimportant to you?

9. Do you notice when he is tired and withdrawn and would like to be left alone?

10. Do you ever take him out in the car, especially if he is disabled, either just for a ride, or to visit some attractive church (for instance)?

11. Have you time to spare for the old when they want to talk, when they simply need a listener?

12. Do you discreetly and tactfully pass over signs of failing health and mental infirmity?

13. Is there a colleague who gets on well with an older member of the community and who takes more concern (or is allowed to take more concern) than the others over his room and clothes?

14. Do you ever think of flowers for his room, tobacco, fruit?

15. Do you invite him out occasionally to the theatre or cinema?

16. Do you take him seriously when he asks for your prayers, or do you dismiss this as a conventional flourish?

17. Do you know what sort of weather he finds disagreeable, and do you try to cheer him up on those days in particular?

18. Do you suspect what your elderly colleague feels when someone of his age has died?

19. Do you send him a new book of your own perhaps,

to amuse or please him, and do you then brace yourself for 'undesirable' reactions?

20. Do you know how your colleagues are coping with old age, with 'death spread over years' (Guardini), with imminent death?

10 A successful death

Of course there is a lot about Teresa of Lisieux and her writings which irritates or simply bores me. If I start to explain, to understand, to translate what I find disagreeable and make it accessible to someone else, it is not altogether clear why I bother to make the effort. There is so much in the world to engage our attention without that sort of long-winded interpretation.

Firstly, however, here is someone who died in the mortal temptation of empty absolute unbelief, and still believed; who believed as she choked with consumption and to whom all the pious fuss of her fellow sisters must have been unutterably empty and painful. Here is someone who died *accepting* as a destructive reality what had been devoutly talked over; what she must have strongly suspected of being a dream world into which a young thing escaped because it was frightened of reality and truth, something that looked as if it belonged to the plush furniture with which the parents of the 'Little Flower' (how touching) crammed their living-room.

Secondly, you could object that a great many people die like that. Whether in a modern aseptic clinic, abandoned by loved ones who slip away helplessly; or under napalm bombs; or — oh, I do not know, people are dying everywhere, and why should I not believe, hoping desperately against hope, that there, if you scrape away from this multifarious death everything that is bourgeois, miserable and pompous, there is still a death in which a person lets himself go, with the courage of faith, hope and love, into the incomprehensible (whom we call God) so that what is really happening is valuable enough to remain for ever? Does it always happen? I don't know. I hope so. I hope it does, although only the misery and the disillusionment of human life effectively appear in death.

What is there about Teresa's death which really interests me, which is special, once we discount the pious ferment surrounding it (to which I have no objection, but which I cannot take so seriously), and for which her environment and even her own petty-bourgeois Christian education were responsible? To this question I give an answer which I imagine will shock most people who are not ecclesially domesticated: because I really trust that *this* death was successful (in the sense just suggested), what I otherwise do not know with the same certainty I trust is true *because* the Church has understood and guaranteed *this* successful death.

Devout *and* undevout turmoil round a death are very ambiguous and of questionable importance. Someone can die a dignified death declaring he is an atheist and with polite thanks reject the pastor's endeavours. Or he can die with the entire panoply of Christian church ceremonial, and want this, and be happy and consoled by it. (Let the Pecksniffs of orthodoxy note that I do *not* equate these two situations.)

We know from the old catechism what *should* result in the case of death, yet in *neither* of these cases can we know what *did* result; not even, in an exact and quite serious sense, when we can say so much that is genuinely edifying about a death (even apart from pious glosses), as is the case with St Teresa. That is because we do not know of anyone *how* he let himself go into the incomprehensible; whether with a willing (beatifying) surrender or with a final protest — which, because of the dignity of freedom, I must also believe is possible. But now the Church tells me that here a death has succeeded as an act of faith. When I say 'Church', I do not mean merely , or even primarily, the official declaration of Rome at the canonization: ultimately, that is no more than an echo of the Church's conviction: of this Church of praying, calling, trusting, and praising Christians.

It does not greatly worry me that the Church's conviction (in that sense) has appeared in such shoddy and infantile forms. That is always the case when a crowd has to do and does something in common. But I trust to those countless Christians for a genuine insight into where that which is genuine and eternal happens. And I accept it confidently as the discernment of spirits (of deaths) which takes place in the Holy Spirit. Once such a death is recognized for what it really and almost impalpably *was*, the statues of little saints with their roses in the niches of many churches can gather dust once again. It is nonetheless true that a person's death succeeds in darkness as the ascent of light, conquering all unbelief and despair.

That is the sort of message I understand. It has the

weight of eternity which comes to every human life. I can also accept it in regard to other people who have died and who show that one can really die with Jesus, accepting unutterable loneliness as God's saving hand. I can also say it of Teresa of Lisieux, who died three years before Nietzsche (and he thought that God — and true man with him — was dead and could not rise again).

The answer has run ahead of the question. The answer can make the question intelligible to Christians yet be a real answer. Roses can be black. They can fall further into the night of death; black roses of hope falling inaudibly, almost indistinguishably; falling into your night, and mine.